BUSES

OF THE ISLE of MAN

1945 ~ present day

RICHARD DAVIS

Published on the Isle of Man by

 Lily Publications, PO Box 33, Ramsey, Isle of Man IM99 4LP

Tel: +44 (0)1624 898446 Fax: +44 (0)1624 898449

E-mail: info@lilypublications.co.uk Web: www.lilypublications.co.uk

INTRODUCTION

It is a great pleasure to introduce Buses of the Isle of Man. The photographs included in the book have been sourced from a number of contributors; many are from well-known local transport photographer Stan Basnett, who in his work with the Isle of Man Highway & Transport Board, eventually becoming Surveyor-General, was often in a position to capture a scene which, all too soon, was to disappear forever.

Stan's photographs are complemented by a selection from other photographers - the late Greg Corrin, Richard Dodge, Barry Edwards, Len Hulme, Tony Wilson's Travel Lens Photographic archives, and a few of my own. Every effort has been made to use the best pictures to hand but, on occasion, it has been necessary to use an odd one which is of lesser quality. Where a particularly historic scene or vehicle is involved, I'm sure you will agree that it is better to have a slightly inferior picture than none at all!

I am indebted to Richard Dodge for his very considerable assistance with the captions. I hope that between us we have eliminated all the errors. If not, I'm sure someone will let us know...

I have been a bus enthusiast for as long as I can remember - longer, probably. When I was three or four years old I was with my mother in a shop on Market Hill in Douglas and, while her attention was momentarily elsewhere, I slipped out and wandered into the nearby Lord Street bus station. Panic must have ensued when I couldn't be found but fortunately, about 20 minutes later, I was returned by a Road Services bus inspector having had an unaccompanied trip round the Onchan route on one of their new red double-deckers.

Some years later, as a police officer, I had quite a lot of involvement with buses. One occasion was a little too close an involvement.....

Aftermath of the accident described in the text - 15th January 1969. Note the A35 van on the far left, with the author standind by the driver's doors. *(Stan Basnett)*

DCT AEC Regent V 5 (677 BMN) is carefully unloaded from the IOM Steam Packet ferry at Douglas harbour in May 1965 - note the yellow front and bonnet top, a feature unique to this and sister 4 (679 BMN). *(Stan Basnett)*

One bitterly cold morning in 1969 I attended an accident in Peel Road, Douglas where an Austin A35 van had overturned in the icy conditions. I parked my new immaculate black Ford Corsair police patrol car well out of harm's way, I thought, on the wide pavement by Hills Meadow. Moments later, DCT Regent V 8122 MN came sailing down the hill from Douglas heading for Spring Valley, with all wheels locked - up onto the pavement, colliding with one of the tall street lamps and shearing it off with a terrific shower of blue sparks. The lamp post came crashing down like a felled tree and headed directly for the Corsair, fortunately hitting the ground a few feet short of the back bumper!

Despite incidents like that, the 1960's were easily my favourite decade - petrol was 5/2d a gallon (26p) and new buses were unloaded from the boat at Douglas by driving them over a couple of hefty planks of wood. Health & Safety? I hear you ask - it hadn't been invented in those days but we seemed to manage somehow....

There used to be an advert outside a cycle shop opposite the end of Pulrose Road in Douglas which read: "Get off that bus - it will never be yours. Come in and buy a bike". Well, the sign was wrong because in later years I progressed to owning and restoring buses but if asked to explain the

1930's scene at Douglas Railway Station. *Right to left* - 1934 Leyland Tiger MN 5071, 1928 Thornycroft BC MN 5468, 1928 ADC MN 5505 and 1927 ADC MN 4927. These were typical of the types in use at the time. The Tiger was new in 1934 and was IOM Road Services' first new bus. It operated until 1951 and was in use as a circus caravan at Lord Street, Douglas between 1955 and 1957 before being scrapped. *(The late Norman Box)*

fascination they hold, I would have difficulty putting it into words. Perhaps the pictures which follow will go some way towards providing an answer?

SETTING THE SCENE

Public motor transport in the Isle of Man started in July 1907 when the Manx Electric Railway commenced a service using two Argus charabancs to connect the Snaefell Mountain Railway Bungalow Station with their Tea Rooms at Tholt-y-Will.

Conventional bus services commenced operation in 1914 when Douglas Corporation Tramways started a service within the town. There was no effective motor bus service outside Douglas until 1927 when several operators started up - Farghers Omnibuses, Manxland Bus Services, Manx Motors and P. Richmond. Fearing a loss of traffic, the Isle of Man Railway Company swiftly started its own

bus operation, later forming a subsidiary company, Isle of Man Road Services, and quickly took over much of the competition. From 1930, until nationalisation, the majority of Island wide bus services were run by IOM Road Services, with those in the Douglas and adjacent areas operated by Douglas Corporation.

Some of the buses inherited by Road Services continued to operate in their previous owners' liveries for a period and, it is thought, several never received the IOM Road Services red and cream scheme - being withdrawn from service before their repaint cycle became due. From a driving perspective, there were other, less immediately obvious differences with some of the acquired older buses, such as the accelerator pedal being placed centrally between the clutch and brake pedals, leading to some exciting moments in an emergency situation.

A Manxland Bus Services vehicle weekly report

At the same time that it was taking delivery of its first Leyland National, IOMRS was continuing to update the double-deck fleet with quality second-hand purchases. Ten relatively youthful Weymann-bodied Leyland Titan PD3A/1s, 72-81 (LMN 72-81), new to Bournemouth Corporation in 1963, arrived on the Island during early Summer 1974, already painted into their new operator's livery. All were to give nine years' further service on the Island. *(Travel Lens Photographic)*

card from the late 1920's warns drivers: "Do not drive fast or race engines. Machines will not stand it" - an injunction which now seems more than a little quaint considering the vastly increased speed and volume of motor traffic on 21st century roads.

Thus the scene is set for this pictorial resumé, which spans the period from the end of the Second World War through to the present day.

Much of this period witnessed interesting and eventful times, initially marked by the resumption of peacetime tourism as a major part of the Island's economy. This was coupled to the need to replace worn-out vehicles, which had to be kept going on a 'make do and mend' basis through the austere war years when deliveries of new vehicles had been restricted to a trickle of utility-bodied Daimler double-decker buses for Douglas Corporation and single-deck Bedfords for DCT and Road Services.

As soon as new vehicles became available both fleets embarked on programmes of considerable fleet renewals with large batches of buses that were to become the mainstay of the respective fleets for over 20 years - at the time Manx buses frequently

had long lives perhaps, in part, reflecting the seasonal nature of much of the operation.

As the 1960's progressed and with changing patterns, both in tourism and leisure time activity, together with the increase in private motoring, the Island's bus operations faced a difficult time. Added to this, rising operational costs forced a need to reduce expenditure in order to retain some routes that were by then marginal at best. Expansion of one-man-operation and the acquisition of numerous second-hand vehicles were notable features by the end of the decade right through until nationalisation. In addition to the used purchases, new single-deck buses were bought by both DCT and IOMRS during the 1970's, the former taking delivery of four Willowbrook light-weight Bedford YRQ's whilst Road Services opted for the trend-setting Leyland National, fourteen of which were delivered before the operation was taken over by the Manx Government, with another six on order.

Many of these later purchases were driven by the long-awaited Manx Government nationalisation of the two operators which had been proposed for

Isle of Man Road Services' Leyland Leopard 97 (697 HMN) when new in June 1967 at King George V Park, Douglas. Equipped with dual-purpose semi-coach seating, the batch (96-98) were also fitted with opening roof-lights and were the first to be delivered in the grey and red livery worn by vehicles used on tour and airport work. *(Stan Basnett)*

many years and which ultimately took place in October 1976 under the Isle of Man National Transport Ltd. banner. In the event, the new operator became little more than a 'nationalised Road Services' operation with many perfectly good former Douglas Corporation vehicles scrapped or sold off cheaply whilst older, and sometimes less suitable, former Road Services buses were retained. Rationalisation of services occurred with many of the former DCT routes being absorbed into the Road Services' network where practical.

This was a period in the Manx economy that had yet to adopt the finance sector with such gusto, and a lack of adequate funding persisted. After the 1977 delivery of the six Leyland Nationals ordered by IOM Road Services, a policy of second-hand purchases was put in place which produced a wide variety of vehicles, some of questionable suitability. Unlike the Road Services second-hand purchases, many of these cast-offs were time-expired, having had arduous lives and in need of major attention, following which some of them saw little service on the Island before being scrapped or sold again. Coupled to the volume of all-over advert buses this

policy did little to enhance the appearance of the fleet, during which time the IOM National Transport Ltd. operation became Isle of Man Passenger Transport Board, combining the Island's nationalised bus and rail networks under one management.

By 1988 and following a further change of management, a return to purchasing new vehicles resumed, although the second-hand market continued to be tapped from time to time. Initially, renewal of the double-deck fleet was targeted with both Northern Counties and all-Leyland Olympians being acquired, introducing an orange and cream livery and the Isle of Man Transport fleetname, greatly enhancing the appearance of the fleet. Later the single-deck fleet was replaced, including the arguably unnecessary purchase of a batch of 25 Marshall-bodied low-floor Dennis Darts in 1997 which effectively ousted very youthful Darts purchased new earlier in the decade.

Towards the end of the century, in 1999, the arrival of David Howard from Eastbourne as Transport Director brought about a further change of livery to red and cream applied in Eastbourne

Other than the six Leyland Nationals ordered by Isle of Man Road Services, the first vehicles acquired by the nationalised operator, in 1979, were fourteen Leyland Atlanteans new to Liverpool Corporation. Allowing the Island introduction of one-person-operation of double-deck vehicles, these one-time trend-setting machines impressed many when new - with engines at the rear, entrance at the front, fluorescent lighting, effective heaters, and an amazing performance. They were also the last buses to be craned off the boat; the introduction of Ro-Ro ferries with the arrival of Manx Line's *Manx Viking* eradicated the need for such an antiquated procedure. Former Liverpool Corporation L746 (CKF 746C), dating from 1965, became 81 (A520 MAN) in the IOM National Transport fleet. *(Richard Davis)*

style, together with a move to a greater percentage of double deck vehicles, with the majority of the single deck fleet being sold. New low-floor double deck buses appeared shortly after his arrival, gaining momentum into the twenty-first century. To speed up the process a number of second-hand double deckers were also acquired as a stop-gap measure, attaining an impressive fleet of smart and tidy vehicles that is the basis of the operation today.

After the departure of David Howard, the purchase of new vehicles became less frequent, but in 2009 a batch of eleven double-deck Wright-bodied Volvo B9TL's was purchased which introduced a further new livery - a carbon copy of East Yorkshire Motor Services' maroon and cream,

together with a new brand, 'Bus Vannin', as the bus arm of the Island's Department of Tourism & Leisure is now known.

"The past is a foreign country, they do things differently there". (L.P. Hartley).

Just how differently is amply illustrated in this fascinating glimpse into the Isle of Man's road transport past. I hope you enjoy it as much as I have.

Richard Davis

The last surviving Leyland Lion on the Island, Massey-bodied MN 5105, which had been new to Manxland Bus Services in 1927. Withdrawn from passenger service in 1951, the Lion is seen at Andreas on 17th March 1966 whilst in use as a tree-lopper, a role it retained until 1967. It is now the oldest surviving complete Manx bus and forms part of Isle of Man Transport's (now Bus Vannin) heritage fleet, awaiting restoration. Andreas airfield control tower is just visible in the right background in the first picture. *(Stan Basnett)*

Another survivor is 1928 Thornycroft BC Forward MN5454, originally operated by Isle of Man Railways and captured in these two views taken in Peel Road, Douglas in September 1964 whilst towing Leyland Titan PD3 XMN 347. Withdrawn from passenger service in 1949, the Thornycroft was used as a towing vehicle until 1969 after which it could be seen on display at Ballaugh Garage. Since restored, it now forms part of the IOM Transport heritage fleet. Photographs of Douglas Corporation buses on tow have proved elusive, perhaps due to the standing instruction that break-downs were to be fixed at the scene if at all possible. Failing that, buses were to be towed only after dark - a matter of civic pride, one assumes. Either that or Cyril Wolsey, who was General Manager from 1932 to 1961, had let it be known he didn't want to see Corporation buses being towed. (Stan Basnett)

Douglas Corporation Tramways (renamed 'Transport' from 1934) purchased several unusual vehicles throughout its existence, arguably the most interesting being the three Vulcans delivered in 1926/1935. The latter delivery comprised two 'low-loaders' registered MAN 123/4, complete with nearside folding screens - similar to the final batch of horse cars purchased the same year, also from the Southport manufacturer. Bedford petrol engines, radiators and gearboxes were installed in 1954, with both vehicles being withdrawn three years later. After withdrawal MAN 123 spent many years as a timekeeper's hut at the Southern 100 race circuit in Castletown before the remains were scrapped circa 1980. (*Travel Lens Photographic/Stan Basnett*)

Isle of Man Road Services more or less standardised on Leyland buses for its requirements, one of the few exceptions being AEC Regal 4, 51 (MN 5108[ii]), dating from 1933. Initially loaned by AEC from April 1934, agreement to purchase the vehicle was reached during late September 1934, the bus remaining in service until 1955. After a period in store, the AEC was sold for non-psv use in 1961 - the photograph being taken, probably inside Laxey depot, during its time in store. *(Vic Nutton - Travel Lens Photographic)*

With the ruins of Peel Castle in the background, the chassis of one of the six Douglas Corporation Leyland KPZ Cubs purchased between 1936 and 1939 finds a new role for the RNLI carrying a 'lifeboat' body. Former DCT 11 (BMN 868) was so fitted between 1959 and 1965, this view being taken in 1964. *(Vic Nutton - Travel Lens Photographic)*

One of Douglas Corporation's new AEC Regents poses with officials in the rear yard at York Road depot during the early 1930's. General Manager Cyril Wolsey is fourth from the left whilst a Tilling-Stevens TS6 can just be seen in the background. *(Isle of Man Newspapers)*

Douglas Corporation Regent 46 (MAN 122) at Lord Street, Douglas in 1953, by which time a route number box had been retro-fitted (only Regent 50 was so equipped from new). Lord Street was, until 1935, a densely packed warren of narrow streets known as the 'Fairy Ground', and was also home to numerous pubs. Transformed into a bus station/air terminal in 1962, this area is today not much different to this 1953 view except that it no longer has a wall with iron railings around it. (*Travel Lens Photographic*)

When Douglas Corporation 1934 AEC Regent 45 (MN 9519) was withdrawn in 1963 it was retained by the Corporation for use by the Water Department until 1968, after which it was sold, becoming a playbus at Ballamona Hospital before being scrapped in 1975. Sister vehicle 46 (MAN 122) was also retained by DCWD after withdrawal for use at sporting events as a ladies' toilet. The bus is seen negotiating Quarter Bridge in 1966, an area radically changed today. (Stan Basnett)

The same Regent at Little Mill, Onchan in January 1964 whilst in use by the Corporation Water Department as a mess hut. (Stan Basnett)

Another DCT Regent, 47 (BMN 866), gets a drink of water behind York Road depot. This bus lasted in service until 1964 when it was sold for use as a hen-house at Greeba Bridge, adjacent to the TT course, until being scrapped during the late 1970's. (Stan Basnett)

A rear view of DCT Regent 47 bound for the White City amusement park as passengers board on Queens Promenade. A member of the local constabulary is visible on the back platform – Police officers on duty were carried free of charge on Corporation buses and it was usual for the policeman to give the bell signals to the driver whilst the conductor went upstairs to collect fares. A range of coaches from the many operators serving the town can be seen to the right, no doubt waiting for their daily clientele. (Len Hulme)

Throughout the 1930's IOM Road Services continued purchasing Leyland vehicles as typified by 1938 all-Leyland Lion LT9 46 (CMN 694). Withdrawn by September 1962, this and sister Lion 45 later found use as immobile campers at Ballacuberagh, Sulby until they were scrapped around the turn of the century. *(Vic Nutton - Travel Lens Photographic)*

The last of ten Douglas Corporation AEC Regents (although later referred to as Regent I, after the introduction of later versions of the chassis by AEC, they were never officially termed as such), passes Palace View Terrace in July 1966 on route 1, heading for Derby Castle. Unlike the earlier DCT Regents 50 (DMN 650), delivered in 1939, was fitted with a diesel engine from new - five others being retro-fitted with second-hand London Transport units in 1954. Internally 50 received ornate lower-deck lighting - the glass being shaped like a flaming torch. *(Stan Basnett)*

15

During the war both Douglas Corporation and IOM Road Services were allocated utility-bodied vehicles by the Ministry of Supply. Both received single-deck Bedford OWBs, whilst DCT also took three Daimler CWA6 double-deckers, with AEC engines, in 1945. Last of the trio, 53 (GMN 242) heads south along Loch Promenade, with the old 'Loch Parade' church in the background. Despite retaining their wooden upper deck seats, all three remained operational until 1970. *(Stan Basnett)*

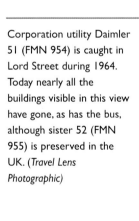

Corporation utility Daimler 51 (FMN 954) is caught in Lord Street during 1964. Today nearly all the buildings visible in this view have gone, as has the bus, although sister 52 (FMN 955) is preserved in the UK. *(Travel Lens Photographic)*

Two single-deck utility Bedford OWBs were acquired by DCT in 1944, arriving in wartime brown livery and becoming 15/16 (FMN 899/900) in the fleet, lasting until 1957. The former rests at Lord Street in 1953 alongside DCT utility Daimler 53 (GMN 242) and IOM Road Services' Leyland Titan PD2 9 (KMN 517). (*Travel Lens Photographic*)

Meanwhile IOM Road Services allocation of wartime utility buses was six similar Duple-bodied Bedford OWB's (a seventh was acquired from Broadbent's Safeway Service, Ramsey in 1950). Unlike DCT, who reduced the seating to 26, IOMRS continued to use the vehicles as 32-seaters until withdrawal in 1966/7. Numbered 26-29/39/40 (GMN 145-50), OWB 27 waits outside Peel Bus Station in 1964. *(Vic Nutton - Travel Lens Photographic)*

After the war, IOM Road Services took delivery of its first double-deckers - twelve Leyland Titan PD1s. When the first bus arrived in 1946, (3, GMN 714), Manx legislation did not permit the use of vehicles with more than 34 seats outside the Douglas area, resulting in the PD1 operating the Onchan circular service with all but eight of its upper deck seats barricaded off, until such time as the law was altered. By the time the other eleven (GMN 775-83/HMN 726/7) were delivered in 1947 all 56 seats were allowed to be used. The PD1s gave around 20-25 years' service with the exception of Titan 12 which overturned in Peel Road, Douglas in August 1958 and was scrapped. GMN 783 is seen at Glen Vine in 1964 and GMN 782 heading from St. John's to Peel in 1963. *(Vic Nutton - Travel Lens Photographic/Stan Basnett)*

A rear view of IOM Road Services' Samlesbury-bodied Leyland Titan PD1 23 (HMN 726) outside Ramsey depot. When withdrawn in 1967, it was converted to an open-top tree-lopper and numbered 122 in the service fleet, being sold in 1977 by IOM National Transport for scrap. *(Stan Basnett)*

Douglas Corporation's first post-war double-deckers, in 1947, were two AEC Regent III RT-type chassis with Northern Counties bodywork, 54/55 (GMN 905/6). The latter passes the Customs & Excise bonded warehouse in Lord Street in 1960 with the now demolished Customs House and St. Barnabas Church in the background. (*Travel Lens Photographic*)

Isle of Man Road Services' post-war single-decker acquisitions commenced with four Leyland PS1 Tiger chassis in 1946, HMN 787-790. Brought to the Island, the chassis were stored for around eighteen months before being returned to the mainland for fitting with Eastern Coach Works' attractive 35-seat rear entrance bodies, returning to the Island during November and December 1947. HMN 790 was one of the last two to enter service in July 1948 and is seen crossing St. John's railway crossing in June 1964, sporting fleetnumber 58. (*Stan Basnett*)

In addition to the Leyland Tigers that finally became operational for IOM Road Services in 1948, a rare Mulliner bus-bodied Bedford OB was also purchased. Given fleetnumber 25 and registration JMN 936, the Bedford is photographed outside Homefield garage in July 1960, having recently operated one of the company's more rural services to Abbeylands. By Road Services' standards the vehicle had but a short life, being withdrawn after only seventeen years, in 1965. *(Vic Nutton - Travel Lens Photographic)*

Ramsey-based Broadbent's Safeway Service's Kirk Michael-Ramsey stage service was acquired by IOM Road Services in October 1950 together with three vehicles. Waveney-bodied Commer Commando 87 (JMN 455) had been new to Hirst Tours, Longwell in 1947, passing to Broadbent the following year. Seen at Circular Road, Douglas in the early 1960's, the Commer was finally withdrawn in 1967 and became one of many buses to end its life as a hen-house on the Island. *(Stan Basnett)*

Another former Broadbent vehicle, KMN 938, a 1949 Armoury-bodied coach seated Bedford OL is seen inside Ramsey depot during 1953. At this time the Bedford was unnumbered, gaining 92 two years later and remaining in service until 1965. All three ex-Broadbent vehicles were stored for between six and nine months after initial acquisition before entering IOMRS service. *(Travel Lens Photographic)*

Duple bus-bodied Bedford OB 30 (LMN 147) is seen parked alongside Ramsey depot building in June 1966. New in 1946, it was originally a Vauxhall Motors experimental chassis and, after bodying as a staff bus, being acquired by IOM Road Services in January 1949, although it didn't enter service for another six months. After withdrawal in 1967 it was converted into a parcels van and numbered 130 before being sold to a local builder. *(Stan Basnett collection)*

Two busy scenes in Peveril Square, Douglas during the early 1950's. In the first picture, passengers queue to board Douglas Corporation Leyland Cub 10 (BMN 256) whilst IOM Road Services' PD2 13 (MMN 11) rounds the corner bound for Lord Street. Looking in the opposite direction, the second picture shows two Douglas Corporation AEC Regent IIIs, a queue of waiting passengers and, to the right, Victoria Pier arcade. *(Stan Basnett collection)*
.

Between 1947 and 1949 Douglas Corporation took delivery of eighteen AEC Regent IIIs as part of a fleet modernisation programme. All received Northern Counties bodywork to a basically standard design, although there were some minor differences between the various batches. Bound for Upper Douglas, Regent 56 (HMN 687) picks up passengers outside Gelling's Foundry in Victoria Street in June 1966. Withdrawn in 1974, the bus was later converted to open-top for the Sporting Carriage Club who had the bus painted blue and white and fitted a bar for hospitality. Re-registered MAN 643J, the second photograph sees the Regent in 1983 at Douglas Railway Station yard shortly before being scrapped. These Regent IIIs, with their pre-selector gearboxes and air brakes, were ideal for town work, their good hill-climbing ability and 7' 6" width enabling them to negotiate what little road traffic there was without difficulty. *(Stan Basnett/Travel Lens Photographic)*

DCT 1948 AEC Regent III 60 (JMN 724) was fitted with a special towing hitch to allow it to move DCT horse cars to and from venues away from the tramway. In April 1976 former South Shields 1883 Metropolitan car 14[ii] is being towed along Peveril Square. At the time this was the only surviving DCT double-deck horse car and had been returned on loan from the Science Museum to allow it to take part in the horse tramway centenary event on 7th August that year. *(Stan Basnett)*

After withdrawal in 1974, sister Douglas Corporation AEC Regent III 58 (HMN 689), from the 1947 batch, was sold to builders Pochin for staff transport and re-registered MAN 691D. Initially operated in DCT livery, the Regent was later repainted white – complete with the Pochin 'elephant' logo applied to the lower deck sides. This scene was captured at Colby in September 1975. 58 was subsequently acquired by Andreas Racing Association and used for several years as a timekeeper's hut at Jurby. After passing to IOM Transport, the bus has now returned to Jurby where it resides in the Transport Museum awaiting restoration. *(Stan Basnett)*

More mundane duties see DCT Regent 60 (JMN 724) travelling up Victoria Street, Douglas in June 1966, at that time a two-way street, on route 18 to Willaston. Passing with the DCT bus operation to IOM National Transport in October 1976, the bus was one of those that IOMNT never operated, despite being allocated fleetnumber 128. *(Stan Basnett)*

With the Villa Marina Colonnade in the background DCT AEC Regent III 62 (JMN 726) is seen on Harris Promenade bound for the Bus Station. Some years earlier the bus collided with Tom King's cycle shop on the corner of Athol Street and Prospect Hill, Douglas due to a mechanical failure, resulting in the chassis needing attention by AEC engineers before returning to service. Douglas Corporation Transport undertook some major maintenance on their buses over the years and made every effort to keep vehicles in service, even to the point of sending an apprentice on a day trip to Liverpool to obtain some vital part to put a bus back on the road. *(Travel Lens Photographic)*

Regent III 66, pictured in June 1966, was part of a batch of eight largely identical vehicles delivered in 1949. There were some detail differences of body style between individual vehicles, including rubber-mounted destination and number screens as shown on 66 (*right*) & 67 (*below*). In later years with DCT another Regent III, 63 (JMN 727), now restored in the UK, was distinguished from the rest of the fleet by having a black-painted radiator surround and 'Treadmaster' flooring fitted the wrong way round, making it difficult for cleaners to sweep out. (*Stan Basnett*)

Somewhat marring the appearance of the rubber-mounted destination and number boxes is the application of yellow paint on DCT AEC Regent III 67 (KMN 838), seen on Queens Promenade, Douglas in June 1966. Half-drop windows common to DCT Regent IIIs are clearly visible - only Regent III 56 was fitted with sliding windows.

Other minor body differences featured on the KMN batch included the side destination box being moved from above the platform to the nearside lower deck window and, from bus 66, reduction in lower deck seating capacity from 26 to 25. (*Stan Basnett*)

Isle of Man Road Services' post-war fleet replacement programme took a major step forward with the purchase of eighteen all-Leyland Titan PD2s in 1949, KMN 500-518. Most of the batch were specially shipped to the Island during February aboard the Atlantic Steam Navigation Co. tank landing craft *Empire Gaelic*, rather than arriving on the Island individually, as was customary at the time. A further four similar buses were delivered in 1950 and 1951. Titan 70 (KMN 500), seen alongside Homefield garage in 1972 shortly before withdrawal, later spent many years on a farm on the Jurby coast road (see picture *middle-left*) until finally scrapped during 2006. (*Tony Wilson - Travel Lens Photographic*)

Lord Street Bus Station during 1971, with IOM Road Services Leyland Titan PD2s, 75/80 (KMN 505/510) and Douglas Corporation AEC Regent V 15 (410 LMN) in view, together with two Road Services Tiger Cubs, in the short-lived grey coaching livery, behind. (*Tony Wilson - Travel Lens Photographic*)

Displaying its classic lines, IOM Road Services' Leyland Titan 81 (KMN 511) is parked at Port Erin in 1964. Withdrawn and sold to dealer Telefilms Transport, Preston in 1970 it was ultimately scrapped, like most others of the batch, although 2 (KMN 504) survives in the Isle of Man Transport heritage fleet. (*Vic Nutton - Travel Lens Photographic*)

In this 1972 view at the rear of Ramsey depot, IOM Road Services' Leyland Titan PD1 122 (HMN 726), ex-bus 23, is shown after conversion as the company's tree-lopper. Although out of use by then, it passed to IOM National Transport in 1976, being sold the following year for scrap. Titan PD2 86 (KMN 516) was withdrawn in 1974 and sold to Lister, Bolton, also for scrap, the following year. (*Tony Wilson - Travel Lens Photographic*)

Some eleven years since delivery of their last Leyland vehicles, Douglas Corporation purchased three Leyland Comets with Park Royal bodywork in 1950, believed to be the only bus-bodied Comets built for the UK market. Withdrawn in 1968, all three found further use on the Island with 21 (KMN 519) since being restored in the UK. Working extended area route 5, the Comet is pictured alongside the Peveril Hotel, Douglas during the early 1950's. *(Stan Basnett)*

Leyland Comet 22 (KMN 520) in the DCT fleet photographed on Queens Promenade in June 1966 and bound for Douglas Bus Station, despite the destination displayed. After withdrawal in 1968 this bus and sister 21 (KMN 519) passed to Parkinson builders for staff transport and, whilst 21 was rescued for preservation, 22 ended its days at Manx Metals scrapyard, Ballasalla, as seen in the view taken in 1981. It was finally scrapped during 1983. *(Stan Basnett/Tony Wilson - Travel Lens Photographic)*

Dozing in the afternoon sunlight inside Peel depot during 1971 are IOM Road Services' Leyland Titan PD1 4 (GMN 775) and Leyland/MCW Olympic 53 (MMN 303). The underfloor-engined Olympic HR40, of integral chassis-less construction, was not universally popular with traditionally conservative bus operators resulting in Road Services, with its fleet of eight purchased in 1950/1 (MMN 296-303), being the main customer for the type. (*Tony Wilson - Travel Lens Photographic*)

En-route to Port Soderick in 1964 IOMRS Leyland Olympic MMN 303 retains its original fleetnumber 85 - the Lambden great renumbering scheme of 1968 saw many IOMRS buses brought together in 'batches', rather than the random way numbers had hitherto been applied. All eight Olympics were withdrawn between 1972 and 1975, MMN 303 succumbing in 1974, passing to Manx Metals scrapyard where it is seen in October 1981 (*next picture*) being finally cut up shortly afterwards. Just one Olympic escaped the cutters' torch, 84 (MMN 302), which has been fully restored. Leyland's highly successful O.600, 9.8 litre diesel engine was to feature in many Manx buses, first appearing in the PD2s and later, Olympic, Royal Tiger, PD3, Leopard and Panther types. (*Vic Nutton - Travel Lens Photographic/Richatd Davis*)

Whilst IOM Road Services opted for Leyland for their first underfloor-engined single-deckers, Douglas Corporation chose their regular chassis supplier, AEC. Two AEC Regal IVs dating from 1950 arrived the following year, gaining numbers and registration marks 30/31 (NMN 201/355). The first, 30, appeared at the 1950 Commercial Motor Show in City of Oxford livery with fleetnumber 730 and registration OJO 730, but was not delivered to Oxford, passing to DCT instead but retaining the distinctive Oxford 'V' on the front dash panel. (Stan Basnett)

Regal 31 had initially been an AEC demonstrator registered VMK 721, and is seen after twenty years' service with DCT emerging into Waverley Road from the rear of York Road depot. Three years later, in 1974, 31 was withdrawn, being sold for scrap in October 1976. (Tony Wilson - Travel Lens Photographic)

Each DCT Regal had bodywork by different manufacturers with a markedly contrasting appearance. A body by Willowbrook of Loughborough was fitted to 30, whilst Park Royal supplied the body for 31. Running out of service the former turns left from Broadway onto Central Promenade later in its service life. *(Tony Wilson - Travel Lens Photographic)*

An earlier view shows Regal 31 on Summerhill Road, Onchan, bound for Victoria Pier in June 1963. *(Stan Basnett)*

Following the large batch of 18 Leyland Titan PD2s, IOM Road Services continued to purchase further similar vehicles, with two batches of two arriving in 1950 and 1951, MMN 11/12 and NMN 361/362. Operating an Onchan circular, 62 (NMN 361) is pictured leaving Lord Street Bus Station in 1964. Withdrawn from service in 1975, as a result of hitting a low bridge, the PD2 was converted into a tree-lopper and allocated number 123 (never carried). It was shipped to the UK via Manx Line on June 25, 1981, together with the seats from Leyland Titan PD3 64 (MN 64) - the vehicle converted into a replacement tree-lopper. The PD2 became a publicity vehicle for Staveley Garage, Shipley. After a succession of owners the bus currently resides with the London Bus Export Co. at Lydney. *(Vic Nutton - Travel Lens Photographic)*

Sister Leyland Titan PD2 66 (NMN 362) was withdrawn from service in 1975 after sustaining fire damage at Homefield garage, passing for use as a hay store at Church Farm, Malew - as seen in this 1983 photograph. Two years later it was scrapped at Foxdale. *(Richard Davis)*

IOM Road Services' Leyland Royal Tiger 91 (NMN 909) pictured in Lord Street during 1953. In the background the fire brigade practice tower is clearly visible and could often be seen in use on a Sunday morning. Two of the Royal Tigers are preserved - one (89) in the UK, the other (88) on the Island. (*Travel Lens Photographic*)

Following the Leyland Olympics, IOM Road Services' next purchase of single-deckers was four all-Leyland Royal Tigers in 1952, 88-91 (NMN 906-9). Last of the batch, 91, pokes its nose out of Homefield garage in July 1960, complete with company crest on the front dash panel. These Leyland-bodied buses used the same engine and running gear as the Olympics but with a separate chassis and were the first eight-foot-wide buses purchased by IOM Road Services. (*Vic Nutton - Travel Lens Photographic*)

With a total of 22 new double-deckers delivered to IOM Road Services between 1949 and 1951 it was another five years before further such buses were required. Three Leyland Titan PD2/20s with Metro-Cammell Orion bodywork, 93-95 (TMN 334-6) appeared in 1956, complete with BMMO 'tin-fronts', the first IOMRS d/d buses to feature an enclosed radiator. 94 is seen in a line of buses at Lord Street Bus Station. *(Vic Nutton - Travel Lens Photographic)*

94 on Main Road, Onchan. From this batch onwards, all IOMRS double-deck deliveries were finished with just a single cream band. *(Stan Basnett)*

Following relaxation in size regulations, Douglas Corporation's first eight-foot wide double-deckers were four Metro-Cammell bodied AEC Regent Vs delivered in 1957, 72-75 (VMN 664-667). With an incorrectly displayed destination, 73 is pictured on Loch Promenade (above) whilst the next picture shows 74 descending Summer Hill. There were some concerns at the time regarding the use of these larger buses on Summerhill. Whilst these proved to be unfounded, the extra width did prove troublesome at times when passing other vehicles, such as at Ellenbrook on the Port Soderick route when one of the eight-footers ended up in a ditch when two buses tried to pass on a narrow section of road. Additionally, passing horse trams on some sections of Douglas promenade was more difficult. Regent 74 carries the letters 'EA' below the front sidelight, which indicated that the bus was one licensed to operate outside the Douglas borough boundary. *(Stan Basnett)*

Two former Douglas Corporation AEC Regent Vs wait between duties at Lord Street Bus Station shortly after nationalisation carrying Isle of Man National Transport fleet numbers and hastily-applied legal lettering. Both buses wear the DCT simplified livery of just one red band above the lower deck windows. A much reduced destination screen is also applied to the open-platform Regent. . *(Tony Wilson - Travel Lens Photographic)*

During July 1957 IOM Road Services took delivery of four Weymann-bodied Leyland Tiger Cubs, 19-22 (WMN 5-8), three of which received red and grey coach livery in 1969, as shown by 20 seen in Lord Street Bus Station during 1971. The batch were renumbered 5-8 on October 5, 1974 and withdrawn on March 31, 1976. A reprieve came after nationalisation when these Tiger Cubs were reinstated to replace former DCT stock not used. WMN 6 was the final member of the batch to remain in service, lasting until 1981 when it was sold for preservation. Fitted with a much smaller engine than their predecessors, a two-speed axle was installed to make up for the lack of power, giving eight forward gears which were useful - when they worked. Unfortunately, after a bit of wear, they tended to slip out of gear, often at crucial moments, leaving the bus devoid of any form of drive. *(Tony Wilson - Travel Lens Photographic)*

Returned to normal bus livery in 1972, the same bus is seen at the rear of Ramsey depot. *(Tony Wilson - Travel Lens Photographic)*

Whilst IOMRS were opting for Leyland Tiger Cubs in 1957, Douglas Corporation, determined to be different as usual, purchased five Guy Otters with distinctive Mulliner 26-seat bodywork, 8-12 (WMN 484-488). Similar in appearance to London Transport's GS class, except for the large destination blinds that characterised DCT buses of the era, the batch remained in service until 1970. Although highly informative, and no doubt much appreciated by visitors to the Island, problems with the large blinds led to a return to smaller screens on later buses. Otter 9 is seen at Peveril Square. *(Stan Basnett)*

Otter 8 leads a rear-entrance AEC Regent V returning from Port Soderick on the Old Castletown Road in this view. Not only did the Otters look different, they also had unusual gears in that first and second gear positions were where you would expect third and fourth to be. After withdrawal, all five Guys found further use in the UK - at least number 9 now being preserved in the UK whilst there may still be other survivors. *(Stan Basnett)*

Former DCT Guy Otter 8 seen in a dealer's yard circa 1977 re-registered UTU 595J and having lost the destination box. After export from the Island the bus initially passed to the Runcorn, Frodsham and District Society for Mentally Handicapped Children whose lettering and logo can be seen applied to DCT livery. *(Travel Lens Photographic)*

DCT returned to Mulliner for the supply of bodywork in 1958, this time on two underfloor-engined AEC Reliances - which were to be unique as Mulliner never bodied any other such buses. Numbered 32/33 (XMN 290/289), the former is pictured passing AEC Regent V 72 (VMN 664) in Lord Street during 1967. After nationalisation the Reliances gained IOM National Transport numbers 190/189 but were short-lived, being soon withdrawn and offered for sale at a reputed £50 for the pair. At that time Island bus preservation had yet to commence and unfortunately both these rare machines passed to a scrap dealer, a sad loss to Manx transport history. *(Tony Wilson - Travel Lens Photographic)*

On the corner of Ridgeway Street and North Quay DCT Reliance 32 (XMN 290) appears to have come into contact with a street light, which has obviously got the worst of the argument. *(Stan Basnett)*

Leyland Motors supplied IOM Road Services with the first three of six new Titan PD3 chassis in 1958, the other three arriving in 1964. The first three, 31-33 (XMN 345-347), were fitted with spartan Metro-Cammell Orion bodywork and, similar to the 1956 delivery of Titan PD2s, the batch were fitted with the Midland Red (BMMO) 'tin-front'. On stand at Lord Street Bus Station with passengers on-board, 32 awaits its departure time. Following withdrawal this bus was acquired for preservation on the Island. Whilst just six new PD3s were purchased, second-hand acquisitions were later to make the chassis a common sight on the Island's roads. *(Stan Basnett)*

A further three Leyland Tiger Cubs were delivered to IOM Road Services in 1961 featuring BET-style Willowbrook bodywork and dual-purpose seating for 41 passengers, 54-56 (3680-3682 MN). The last of the trio has just passed over the Isle of Man Railway level crossing in Station Road, St. John's. *(Stan Basnett)*

One of the three 1961 Leyland Tiger Cubs has been reacquired by Isle of Man Transport as part of the vintage fleet, although it remains in 'as acquired' condition. Emerging on tow from the former Homefield garage paintshop on 18th February 2009, Cub 54 begins its journey to the Jurby Transport Museum. *(Richard Davis)*

Douglas Corporation bought its first front-entrance AEC Regent Vs in 1964, again featuring Metro-Cammell Orion bodywork. Numbered 1-3 (8122-4 MN), and with semi-automatic gearboxes, the buses were reliable performers lasting well into the nationalised era. Onchan Park, outside the borough boundary, is the setting for this view of Regent 1, which was to become the final operational former Douglas bus with IOM National Transport, being withdrawn in 1982. *(Stan Basnett)*

AEC Regent V 3 (8124 MN) sits opposite the Corporation's York Road depot during 1971. In line with DCT policy, the wheel chock can clearly be seen positioned under the front offside wheel. When parking on inclines, drivers were required to chock a wheel to stop a vehicle rolling away in the event of brake failure - something that pre-selector and semi-auto gearboxes will not prevent. (*Travel Lens Photographic*)

DCT AEC Regent 4 (679 BMN) turns right onto the Old Castletown Road at the bottom of Oak Hill, returning to Douglas from Port Soderick. In addition to changing from large to minimal frontal destination screens, those hitherto fitted to the rear were omitted altogether on the front-entrance Regent Vs. White City amusement park was a regular advertiser on DCT buses being a popular holiday venue on Onchan Head. *(Stan Basnett)*

In 1964 IOM Road Services took delivery of its next, and last, new Leyland Titan PD3s, 59-61 (6-8 MAN). Metro-Cammell Orion bodywork is again fitted, but the radiator enclosure differs from the earlier batch, being of the 'St. Helens' style so named after the operator who first adopted it. All three buses were later renumbered and re-registered at least once, ultimately becoming 69/67/68 (69/67/68 UMN). Seen climbing out of Union Mills en route to Peel, 60 was sold for preservation when finally withdrawn by IOM National Transport and has since been reacquired as part of the vintage fleet. Should anyone wish to restore a Road Services bus, the paint used by the operator was Tekaloid 'bright red' and 'broken white'. *(Stan Basnett)*

Two more AEC Regent Vs were added to the Douglas Corporation fleet in 1967, with Willowbrook of Loughborough supplying the bodywork. 4/5 (679/677 BMN) were distinctive in featuring yellow painted bonnets and radiator surround panels upon delivery. Unlike IOMRS, who used Tekaloid paints, DCT opted for Joseph Mason - 'primrose' yellow and 'deep Mason's red' being the colours. Regent 4 is seen on Queens Promenade in June 1966 whilst carrying the yellow front; these were later repainted to conform to standard appearance. This bus was the first front-entrance Regent V withdrawn by IOM National Transport, in 1981, and was exported to the UK for preservation; unfortunately it was burned-out on Wallasey docks. Meanwhile the remains of sister bus 5 were cut up at the Point of Ayre scrapyard. *(Stan Basnett)*

Douglas Corporation AEC Regent 50 (DMN 650) passes E.B. Christian's garage on North Quay, Douglas (which featured a turntable inside) whilst working route 25 from Douglas Head, despite the destination shown. This area has changed almost out of recognition over the last twenty years and at this point is now a single carriageway and pedestrian area. (*Travel Lens Photographic*)

The same bus during 2004. Regent 50 is preserved on the Island, although requiring further restoration, and is believed to be the only surviving DCT pre-war Regent. Similar 46 (MAN 122) was recorded as preserved in the UK but there have been no reports for many years and it may well have been scrapped. (*Richard Davis*)

Isle of Man Road Services' 28 (GMN 147), a Duple utility-bodied wartime Bedford OWB parked in front of Ramsey garage with gleaming paintwork, perhaps following a recent visit to the paintshop. After withdrawal the OWB spent many years on a farm at Ballanicholas until it disintegrated on site during the early 1990's. *(Vic Nutton - Travel Lens Photographic)*

In the early-morning murky gloom at Lord Street Bus Station IOM Road Services Leyland Titan PD1 3 (GMN 714) is seen parked alongside the centre island, which contained the offices and airport terminal. A Leyland Royal-Tiger can be seen in the distance. *(Geoff Lumb - Travel Lens Photographic)*

On 4th November 1985 second-hand Leyland National 13 (MAN 13A) entered service for IOMPTB in Douglas Corporation livery applied to commemorate almost 65 years of bus operation between 1914 and 1976. When this bus was scrapped National 29 (MAN 29N) was chosen as a replacement to carry the livery. With appropriately set destination, National 29 emerges from the former bus wash at Douglas railway yard - this part of the yard has since been redeveloped and now forms part of a supermarket car park.

Meanwhile a commemorative IOM Road Services livery was applied to Leyland Lynx 1 (BMN 401T) shortly after it arrived in January 1990, a livery it was to retain for the majority of its service life. The Lynx poses for the camera at Douglas railway yard on September 7, 1991 (lower). *(The late Greg Corrin/Richard Dodge)*

Former Ribble Motor Services Marshall-bodied Leyland Leopard 4 (F458 MAN) at the Sound, at the time retaining NBC poppy red livery. One of a batch of ten acquired by IOM National Transport during 1979/80, the last remained in service until 1985. Sisters 7 & 10 are preserved on the Island while 6 has been 'cannibalised' for spares. (*Travel Lens Photographic*)

Now preserved, IOMRS Thornycroft BC Forward 13 (MN 5454) is captured in an earlier time flanked by two number 28s - Austin delivery van from the IOMRS parcel van fleet on the left and Duple-bodied Bedford OWB GMN 147 on the right. (*Geoff Lumb - Travel Lens Photographic*)

An early 1950's shot of Loch Promenade taken from the top of the Villa Marina Colonnade, with tourists, horse trams and buses all very evident. DCT GF Milnes 1902 horse car 40 advertises a 4d fare, the equivalent of 1.66 pence in today's decimal coinage. At this time, the Island retained a thriving tourist industry with many visitors exploring Island-wide attractions by public transport. In mid-Summer Douglas beach was crammed with deck-chairs and getting from the promenade to the sea was a matter of picking your way carefully between them. Felice's ice cream kiosk, seen between the two buses, would often generate queues as far as the war memorial, out of sight to the right of the picture. Note the drinking facilities for humans and donkeys on the right of the picture. *(Len Hulme)*

Not the best of photographs but included for rarity value is this colour view of Douglas Corporation Tilling-Stevens TS6 29 (MN 5500) with Northern Counties bodywork. New in 1928, the bus is pictured on Queens Promenade during 1949 - its last year of operation. The only surviving former DCT Tilling-Stevens is 10 (MN 2615), which exists as a chassis and was more recently on display at the London Transport Museum in Covent Garden. *(Geoff Lumb - Travel Lens Photographic)*

Last in a long line of AEC Regents for DCT, as well as being the final AEC double-deck chassis, 15 (410 LMN) is seen whilst being unloaded from an IOMSPCo. ferry during December 1968. It was to become the last new double-deck bus the Island was to see for twenty years. *(Stan Basnett)*

Whilst the Island doesn't usually suffer from the extremes in weather, being situated in the Gulf Stream, occasionally snow does fall, making movement difficult. DCT Regent V 1 (8122 MN) appears to be having a problem on the climb up Prospect Hill, Douglas during January 1968 as it passes the former Dumbells Bank building. The failure of the bank at the turn of the twentieth century was to have a significant effect on much of the Manx transport systems of the day. *(Stan Basnett)*

Isle of Man Passenger Transport Board Leyland National 20 (MAN 20D) suffers a similar fate between East and West Baldwin during February 1985. *(Stan Basnett)*

Isle of Man National Transport 33 (MAN 33N), the last of the new Leyland Nationals delivered to the Island, waits between duties on the 'patch' in front of Cambrian Place opposite Douglas Bus Station. This batch of six buses 28-33 (MAN 28-33N) were ordered by IOM Road Services prior to the 1976 nationalisation but delivered to IOM National Transport in 1977. *(Stan Basnett)*

From the early 1980's a vast number of Manx buses were to feature all-over advertising for a wide range of sponsors. Whilst the designs of some were less appealing a number were in effect impressive works of art, such as the Laxey Heritage Trust scheme applied to Leyland National 27 (MAN 27H). The National, which was historically significant being the last vehicle delivered to Isle of Man Road Services in 1976, unloads passengers at Castletown Square on September 30, 1995. *(Richard Dodge)*

Three new attractive Optares, 41-43 (MAN 41-43H), were purchased during 2000 but despite their modern appearance no further examples were bought. Optare 43 (MAN 43H) is pictured in Douglas railway yard on April 6th, 2007. *(Barry Edwards)*

During the 'Howard' era just one new single-deck bus was purchased, effectively highlighting the importance of the double-decker to the Manx operation. East Lancs special narrow-bodied Alexander Dennis Dart SLF 82 (MN 1082), delivered during 2005, was also finished with a cream front panel, giving a rather unusual appearance. Older Dart 34 was similarly treated but swiftly repainted into standard livery. Dart 82 is seen at Douglas Railway Station bus park on April 4th, 2006. *(Barry Edwards)*

An unusual purchase for a municipal operation was the Bedford VAS1, Douglas Corporation taking delivery of two with Duple Midland bodywork in 1966, 6/7 (899/900 EMN). Bus 7, pictured alongside the former cable tramway winding house at the rear of York Road depot, is still extant in the north of the Island. *(Tony Wilson - Travel Lens Photographic)*

Sister DCT Bedford VAS1 6 (899 EMN) is seen on the public weighbridge outside E.B. Christian's garage at Bridge Road, Douglas in 1966. Most of the buildings visible in the background have since disappeared. *(Stan Basnett)*

Throughout the Sheard era, IOM Road Services acquired few second-hand buses, but following his death and the appointment of W.T. Lambden such purchases were to become more frequent, commencing in 1967 with the acquisition of seven ex-Aldershot & District 1956 Strachan-bodied Dennis Falcons, 23-29 (23-29 HMN). Sporting a non-standard fleetname 25, pictured at King George V Park, was one of the vehicles to be repainted red before entering service - several of the batch operated in their former green livery until 1969 when the paintshop could deal with them. Falcon 29 was sold for preservation after withdrawal and has since returned to the UK where its restoration to original A&D condition is nearing completion. *(Stan Basnett)*

Isle of Man Road Services dabbled with coaching in the late 1960's/early 'seventies, buying new coaches and painting some existing single-deckers in grey and red coach livery. Following rationalisation in 1971/2, most of the coaches, including Duple Commander-bodied Leyland Leopard 36 (36 LMN) on the left of the picture, were transferred to Tours (IOM) which had been purchased jointly by Road Services/Corkill's in whose green and cream livery it is seen at Douglas Bus Station. *(Travel Lens Photographic)*

Last of the line - the final Douglas Corporation double-deckers were two further Willowbrook-bodied AEC Regent Vs, 14/15 (409/10 LMN), delivered in 1968. These differed slightly from the earlier Regent Vs, being of the 3D2RA type with 11.3 litre engines and another variation in livery, having a yellow radiator surround panel whilst reverting to a red bonnet top. In the company of Guy Otter 8 (WMN 484) Regent 14 is parked in front of Cambrian Place, the differing destination styles being most evident. (*Travel Lens Photographic*)

AEC Regent 15 (410 LMN) was not only the final Douglas Corporation double-decker but also the last double-decker built by AEC. Following a time in the UK after withdrawal, it has now returned to the Island and is part of IOM Transport's vintage fleet now resident at the Jurby Transport Museum. All four Regent Vs delivered with yellow fronts were repainted as shown in this view taken in IOMT days at the former IOM Railway Douglas yard depot. (*Stan Basnett*)

With nationalisation under discussion, Douglas Corporation turned to the second-hand market for its next purchases, with eight Duple-bodied Leyland Tiger Cubs, new to Lancashire United Transport in 1957/8, being acquired in 1970, 34-41 (227/29-34/38 UMN). Tiger Cub 36 is seen at the Port Soderick turning circle, having worked a 15 service from Douglas during 1971. Like the rest of the batch, it was scrapped after withdrawal. *(Tony Wilson - Travel Lens Photographic-*

Tiger Cub 38 (232 UMN) sits in a line up of vehicles on the Corporation bus parking area at Cambrian Place, Douglas. Although allocated IOM National Transport fleet numbers following nationalisation, just two of the batch (35/41) were operated, one very briefly, neither having the new numbers applied. *(Tony Wilson - Travel Lens Photographic)*

In a complete change of chassis supplier, following their availability on the open market again, IOM Road Services took delivery of four Bristol RE coaches during 1970/71, 37-40 (37/38 UMN, 39/40 WMN). The first two carried Duple bodywork with the 1971 batch receiving Plaxton's, whilst Leyland engines were fitted to all four, some of the first vehicles in the country to be so treated. Their Island life was plagued by overheating problems and all were sold in 1973 - 39/40 having been loaned to Tours (IOM) for the 1972 summer season. The last of the four, 40, is seen on the climb to the Island's only mountain, Snaefell, and has recently been acquired by the respected Essex operator Talisman of Great Bromley for restoration, now registered SGF 483L. *(Stan Basnett)*

An interior view of the Bristol RE 40 (40 WMN) in June 1971 with IOM Road Services' General Manager, William Lambden, seated on the right, with Dick Craine, Secretary to the Commissioners standing, on an evaluation trip with newly-formed Road Traffic Commissioners. *(Stan Basnett)*

Bristol RE 40 (40 WMN) captured on the TT course at the 33rd milestone bend, travelling towards Douglas. *(Stan Basnett)*

Before the advent of Ro-Ro vessels, transporting larger vehicles to the Island was more time-consuming and cumbersome, vehicles often being carried across the ship's forepeak ahead of the superstructure. In the next series of photographs the transportation process, rarely witnessed by the general public, is depicted, providing an interesting insight into how things were done years ago. The first picture shows a glossy paint finish on a Douglas Corporation AEC Regent I about to be driven off the ship at Douglas during the early/mid 1930's. (Stan Basnett collection)

Right & Below: Last of the Douglas Corporation AEC Regents, 1939 Northern Counties-bodied 50 (DMN 650), is seen on board the IOM Steam Packet vessel and being driven onto the pier at Douglas. There are a number of minor differences between this and earlier Regents, including unshaded lettering & less elaborate lining-out, slotted air vents and the absence of a projecting horn trumpet. (Stan Basnett collection)

At the Battery Pier in Douglas the Harbour Board's steam crane is busy unloading former Stratford Blue/Midland Red (BMMO) Leyland Titan PD3s in this sequence from January 1972. IOM Road Services acquired fifteen such buses from Midland Red during 1971/1972, introducing forward-entrance double-deckers into the fleet. Despite the age of some of the vehicles they were to feature on Manx roads for a number of years, the last not being withdrawn until September 1983. *(Stan Basnett)*

Isle of Man Steam Packet vessel *King Orry* (IV) enters Douglas Bay on July 27, 1964 with either Road Services new Metro-Cammell-bodied Leyland Titan PD3 7 or 8 MAN on board. *(Stan Basnett)*

In this May 1965 view *King Orry* (IV) arrives at Douglas with AEC Regent V 5 (677 BMN). *(Stan Basnett)*

This manoeuvre had to be done within four minutes on a rising or falling tide as the changing tide level would soon make the angle of the ramp impossible to negotiate. *(Stan Basnett)*

More commonly, buses were shipped individually as shown here in this 12th December 1968 view of TSS *Manxman* (II) approaching Douglas with a Corporation Regent V across the bows. *(Stan Basnett)*

These two photographs, taken on 2nd April 1976, depict Isle of Man Road Services' trend-setting Leyland National 22 (MAN 22H) being craned on to Douglas harbourside from the Steam Packet cargo boat, **Conister**. In total IOM Road Services ordered twenty Leyland Nationals, 14-33 (MAN 14A, 15-20D, 21-27H, 28-33N) over a four-year period, although the last six were to be delivered to IOM National Transport following nationalisation in 1976. *(Stan Basnett)*

Prior to entering passenger service, all new buses had to undergo a Manx psv examination, with vehicles being presented to the then Isle of Man Highway & Transport Board. Awaiting test at the Highway Board yard at Quarter Bridge, later replaced by a new facility at Ballafletcher, is IOM Road Services' first Leyland National, 14 (MN 9514) new in 1974. After only a few weeks service the vehicle was re-registered MAN 14A. Despite some problems with the type, most notably the often troublesome 510 engine and the saloon heating arrangement where hot air was forced down from above with obvious consequences, the Leyland National did introduce a level of both passenger and driver comfort previously unseen on the Island's buses, lasting in service longer than many had originally forecast. Throughout the 1980's they were to form the backbone of the fleet and were often relied upon when other types were failing on an almost daily basis. (Stan Basnett)

By 1979 all of IOM National Transport's single-deck buses were one-person-operated whilst double-deckers remained crew operated, i.e. with separate driver and conductor. To introduce o-p-o into the double-deck fleet a batch of 14 ex-Merseyside PTE Leyland Atlanteans was acquired - 75-88 (A686, 515-23 MAN, C56-58/55 MAN). New in 1965/66 the Metro-Cammell bodies on these buses were amongst the first to challenge preconceived ideas on how a rear-engined double-decker should be bodied, introducing an innovative style and level of interior design not previously seen. MPTE L714 (CKF 714D), which became IOM National Transport 76, arrives at Douglas harbourside during February 1979 - these buses being the last to be craned off ships following the advent of Manx Line's Ro-Ro service operated by their excellent vessel *Manx Viking*. *(Richard Davis)*

One of the 14 ex-Merseyside Leyland Atlanteans was used as a source of spares, despite the original intention - it had been allocated fleetnumber and registration 85 (C56 MAN). This July 1981 photograph, taken at Douglas Railway Station yard, shows Atlantean (L725), together with Leyland Titan PD3s 60/65/66 (MN 60/65/66), all awaiting scrapping. Later second-hand Atlantean purchases were also used as donor vehicles including ex-Tyne & Wear PTE 721 (GBB 521K) - to have been IOM Passenger Transport Board (as IOMNT had by then become) 58 (R171 MAN) until it was found to have a cracked chassis - and six former Merseyside 'Jumbo' Atlanteans that were dismantled on behalf of IOMPTB in Liverpool. *(Richard Davis)*

An interior view of the former Douglas Corporation York Road depot, originally the Upper Douglas cable car depot, showing IOM National Transport's 1963 ex-Stratford Blue Northern Counties-bodied Leyland Titan PD3 57 (MN 57), one of three such buses converted to open-top format during 1979, primarily for use between Douglas & Onchan Heads. A revised livery incorporating a greater area of white was applied to these vehicles, together with an attractive 'cartoon' of the bus on the rear. Some fairly major overhauls and rebuilds were undertaken in the bus works including complete engine strip-downs and rebuilds. However, the engines didn't always go back to where they had come from and records show at least one example of a PD3 engine being fitted to an Olympic and an Atlantean engine going into a PD3. *(Tony Wilson - Travel Lens Photographic)*

The intended open-top conversion of the fourth of IOM National Transport's 57-60 batch of Leyland Titan PD3s - 60 (MN 60) - never took place, the scheme being halted before the bus was taken into the workshops. Waiting at the Ramsey stand in Douglas Bus Station 60 shows off its exposed radiator and off-side illuminated advert panel, popular for a short period during the 1960's. In the background sister Titan 64 (MN 64), complete with 'St Helens' front, can be seen. *(Tony Wilson - Travel Lens Photographic)*

At the same time that IOM Road Services were taking delivery of the modern Leyland National, Douglas Corporation purchased four unusual (for a municipal fleet) Willowbrook bus-bodied Bedford YRQs, 16-19 (MAN 51/52/138/139B). Never popular, following transfer to IOM National Transport their service life was short with the buses being withdrawn during 1980, despite being only 5/6 years old. DCT 16 is seen on display at the 1974 Commercial Motor Show at Earl's Court prior to arrival on the Island. After withdrawal all were sold for further use in the UK, MAN 51B being re-registered FWB 179V with the Walsall Area Health Authority. *(Travel Lens Photographic)*

Last survivor of the L700 class of ex-Merseyside PTE Leyland Atlanteans is C57 MAN - IOM National Transport 86, now preserved on the Island but seen when still in service in Lord Street, Douglas having arrived from Peel. Liverpool Corporation (in the days prior to the formation of Merseyside PTE) took delivery of 380 such buses between 1962-1967 (L500-L879) with just four still known to exist, including IOMNT 86, which was formerly L728 (CKF 728C) new in 1965. *(Tony Wilson - Travel Lens Photographic)*

Metro-Cammell's curved rear panel line can clearly be seen in this view of IOMNT Leyland Atlantean 79 (A518 MAN) taken in the psv inspection bay at the IOM Highway Board Depot at Quarter Bridge in March 1979. *(Stan Basnett)*

Two unusual acquisitions were made in 1979 when a pair of former Wallace Arnold Plaxton-bodied Leyland Leopard coaches were added to the IOMNT fleet, 89/90 (A814/5 MAN). Whilst they were to prove useful on occasion, a conductor was required when operating a stage service as the coaches had manually-operated doors. The second of the duo is seen at Douglas Bus Station in front of Atlantean 38. *(The late Greg Corrin)*

By 1979/1980 many of IOM National Transport's older single-deck buses had become time expired resulting in the purchase of a batch of ten former Ribble Leyland Leopards with BET-style Marshall bodywork, new in 1966. Many required considerable attention, such as new body cross-members, with some having relatively short operational Island lives, although 3 (F808 MAN), seen outside Peel Bus Station, lasted until 1985, albeit renumbered 13 during its final months.*(The late Greg Corrin)*

Sixteen ex-Tyne & Wear PTE Alexander panoramic-bodied Leyland Atlanteans were purchased by IOM National Transport during 1981/2, 54-69 (R167-72, N870-79 MAN). Many wore the wide range of all-over advert liveries that the fleet was to be renowned for during the 1980's including 65 (N875 MAN) seen entering Douglas Bus Station. New in 1972 as Tyneside PTE (the forerunner to TWPTE) 680 (GBB 516K), the bus later served with the IOM Karting Club before being returned to the UK where it has been fully restored to Tyne & Wear condition complete with reinstatement of the centre door. (*Travel Lens Photographic*)

Between 1982-1984 IOM Passenger Transport Board acquired 35 (29 for service, 6 for spare parts) former Merseyside PTE Leyland Atlantean PDR2/1s dating from 1970/1971. Known as 'Jumbos' due to their 33' length and high seating capacity, four of them initially entered service on the Island in MPTE green and cream livery. One of the last to arrive on the Island, 76 (MAN 5623) departs Douglas Bus Station working the Ramsey trunk service, known for many years as route 15, wearing the then red and white livery. (*Travel Lens Photographic*)

Leyland National 19 (MAN 19D[i]) was involved in an accident at Baldrine on 10th April 1985 resulting in the IOMPTB vehicle leaving the road and rolling onto its side - trees stopped the National from slipping further down the bank. (*Stan Basnett*)

Structural strength of the National design meant that, despite a lot of panel damage, the bus retained its shape reasonably well.

Amazingly few suffered injury as a result of the crash, but recovery of the bus was not an easy process, the use of a crane being required. Surprisingly the Leyland National was subsequently returned to Leyland Motors via Manx Line's vessel *Manx Viking*, where it was declared not worth repairing. Perhaps even more surprising was that it was felt worth shipping the bus back to the Island - where it was sent for scrap. *(Stan Basnett)*

Top Left: Apparently intended to be the forerunner of a large batch of smaller midi-buses for both IOMPTB and other Government departments who employ buses as non-psvs, this former 1974 Greater Manchester PTE Pennine-bodied 19-seat Seddon Pennine 4 was to be unique in the Manx fleet and no further examples appeared. Numbered 81 (1063 MAN - formerly GMPTE 1727, XVU 357M) the bus arrived in May 1985, entering service during August. Its short wheelbase made for an uncomfortable ride on the uneven Manx country roads and it saw little use before being withdrawn during July 1986 and converted into a luggage carrier before its later sale. Captured at Port Erin during April 1986. *(Richard Dodge)*

Top Right: Replacing the former Ribble Leyland Leopards in the IOM Passenger Transport Board fleet were newer former Borough of Preston Transport Seddon and Marshall-bodied Leyland Panthers, including 1 (MAN 7656 - ex Preston 235, RTF 435L) seen at Douglas Bus Station. Thirteen such buses were purchased between 1982-1984 and were, perhaps, not the most popular buses with drivers as the low driving position made it difficult to obtain a clear view to the left when emerging from sharply angled junctions. Some Panthers also had ramped floors, which did not endear them to passengers. The batch had a relatively short life on the Island, the first being withdrawn after just three months' use and all had gone by 1986. *(Tony Wilson - Travel Lens Photographic)*

Below: By 1985, and despite their short Manx service, replacement of the Leyland Panthers became necessary and, taking advantage of the forthcoming UK bus industry deregulation scheduled for the following year, IOMPTB were able to acquire 20 second-hand 1973-1976 Leyland Nationals, all bar three being of the shorter 10.3m length with dual-doors, from South Yorkshire PTE. Delivered to the Island between November 1985 and September 1986, the Nationals arrived still wearing SYPTE brown and cream livery, being repainted prior to entry into service. The three 11.3metre Nationals were new to East Kent, but arrived on the Island via National Welsh, in whose livery NFN 67M is seen at Douglas railway yard on October 12, 1985. Once repainted the bus became IOMPTB 82 (2219 MAN). *(Richard Dodge)*

In the following sequence, former SYPTE Leyland National 2750 MAN is captured at the Ballafletcher vehicle testing centre prior to entry into IOMPTB passenger service in February 1986. Formerly registered JDT 435N, it would become 79 in the Manx fleet. In the first view, radiator fan drive and battery security are checked. The second view shows vehicle examiner Selwyn Taggart examining the vehicle whilst the author can just be glimpsed at the left edge of the picture, probably conducting HGV driving tests. *(Stan Basnett)*

Top Left: It is not common to see photographs of a bus undergoing its examination and these views illustrate some of the many checks that are undertaken, such as the vehicle's brake efficiency being tested by Selwyn Taggart. *(Stan Basnett)*

Top Right: Underneath the National with Selwyn Taggart checking for air and fluid leaks. *(Stan Basnett)*

Headlight beams being tested by examiners Norman Radcliffe and Eddie McEvoy. *(Stan Basnett)*

During 1985/1986 IOMPTB acquired 15 ageing Park Royal-bodied Leyland Atlantean AN68s from Greater Manchester PTE, presumably as replacements for the non-arrival of ex-GMPTE Seddon midi-buses. These Atlanteans replaced those acquired from Tyne & Wear PTE four years earlier, but were only a year newer, resulting in the average age of the fleet increasing even further. Like many of the second-hand purchases of that era, these Atlanteans had relatively short Island lives ranging from 21 months to 4 years, and included one bus that, on failing in service, was towed directly to the scrapyard. Two of the batch are seen on January 11, 1986 at Douglas Railway Station yard awaiting their turn to be prepared for service. XJA 505L would become number 68 (2695 MAN). *(Richard Dodge)*

Below Left:: Former GMPTE Atlantean 7137 (XJA 528L) undergoes overhaul at Homefield depot in October 1986 prior to repainting into IOMPTB red and white livery where it would become 65 (4288 MAN). *(Stan Basnett)*

Below Right:: Following withdrawal and storage for several months, one-time Greater Manchester PTE Park Royal-bodied Leyland Atlantean 67 (2699 MAN) passed to the IOM Department of Transport during October 1989 for use as a tree-lopper, the last Island bus to date so converted. Painted in all-over yellow, the Atlantean is seen at Mines Road, Laxey during February 1992 - it wasn't to survive that much longer. *(Richard Dodge)*

A change of direction, livery and name took place following the arrival of Robert Smith as Transport Executive with new buses being bought in 1988, the first for eleven years. The fleet, now named Isle of Man Transport, was finished in a pleasant orange and cream scheme, the all-Leyland Olympians 83-87 (BMN 83-87G) new in 1988 being amongst the first to sport the livery. The sixth member of the batch, 88 (BMN 88G[iii]) was fitted with coach seats and carried an all-cream livery with a painting of the world-famous Laxey Wheel on the offside. These buses were to be some of the first bodied by Leyland since 1954 and suffered from some teething problems and late deliveries. To aid IOMT, Leyland loaned a couple of demonstrator buses until delivery could be completed, which, surprisingly, were also registered BMN 88G. First to arrive with IOMT was an unregistered Olympian demonstrator, which became BMN 88G[i], followed by a Leyland Lynx, which had been registered E709 MFV and which became BMN 88G[ii] before delivery of the proper BMN 88G[iii]. The loaned Olympian is seen on Victoria Pier (above), whilst the Lynx waits at Douglas railway yard during November 1988 having just worked from Ramsey (below). Over the next few years numerous demonstrator buses were loaned to IOMT for evaluation. (*Tony Wilson - Travel Lens Photographic/Richard Dodge*)

The 'real' BMN 88G, pictured at Castletown Railway Station whilst working a private hire (the wedding of Stan Basnett's youngest daughter) on 31st May 1989; the Laxey Wheel painting can clearly be seen. When delivered these six buses had side sliding window openers, but were subsequently returned to Leyland's Workington factory, in some instances more than once, and had these replaced with the hoppers visible in this photograph. *(Stan Basnett)*

Prior to the arrival of the Leyland Olympians the new livery was first applied to ex-MPTE 'Jumbo' Leyland Atlantean 75 (MAN 5720), although the layout finally adopted differed slightly. 75 is captured in Douglas Aquadrome car park during November 1988, prior to IOM Transport fleetnames being applied. *(Richard Dodge)*

A further thirteen Leyland Olympians (58-70, BMN 58-64V, BMN 65/66P, BMN 67-70M) were added to the IOMT fleet between 1989/1990, with bodywork by Northern Counties, once Douglas Corporation's favoured body manufacturer. All were delivered in IOMT's orange and cream livery, but three would later receive an attractive, though short-lived, red and cream livery in the autumn of 1999. One of the trio, 64, sits over the steam-cleaning pit at Douglas Railway Station yard on February 19, 2000. *(Richard Dodge)*

Not long into the 'Smith' era a number of single-deck demonstrator buses were evaluated with a view to upgrading Isle of Man Transport's single-deck fleet. Many were midi-buses although one had a seating capacity just under that of a short Leyland National - Dennis Dart CMN 12A. On loan from Carlyle Bus, Birmingham, the Dart initially entered service on 12th January 1991 in all-over cream as IOMT 41, although it was later renumbered 12 and received the new single-deck livery and lettering for the then new Ramsey 'Skipper' town service as shown in this view at the town's depot on 8th September that year. Whilst the Dart was to feature heavily in the Manx fleet, no Carlyle-bodied versions were to be purchased. *(Richard Dodge)*

Ending the long line of 95 second-hand Leyland Atlanteans commencing in 1979 was a batch of 15 Alexander-bodied AN68A/1R's acquired from Stagecoach during 1991/1992. Carrying Alexander dual-door bodywork the buses had been new in 1978/1979 to City of Portsmouth Transport Department and arrived on the Island carrying a variety of liveries. Some had been converted to single-door configuration prior to their Island arrival with just one vehicle later converted by IOMT, all others retaining the centre exit. Although 15 buses were to be obtained (34-48 - CMN 34-48C), one, 45, was destroyed by fire prior to dispatch and was not replaced, just fourteen being delivered to the Island. UOR 329T, later IOMT 43 (CMN 43C), is seen just after arrival at Douglas railway yard, one of those not repainted in the UK. *(The late Greg Corrin)*

After updating the double-deck fleet, IOMT commenced replacing older single-deckers, purchasing 22 Reeve Burgess/Plaxton Dennis Darts between 1992-1995 of both 9 and 9.8 metre lengths. Dart 9, seen in Sulby Glen whilst working a private hire for the Manx Electric Railway Society on 31st May 1992, was one of the shorter batch numbered 3-13/71 (CMN 103-8L, CMN 9-13H, CMN 71P). These Darts were to be withdrawn prematurely, being surplus to requirements following the return to greater use of double-deckers at the end of the decade. *(Richard Dodge)*

During 1993 IOMT purchased five former Kingston-upon-Hull East Lancs-bodied Dennis Dominators, 49-53 (CMN 49-53T), new in 1986. With ex-IOMRS Leyland Titan PD2 XMN 346 to its left, Dominator 51 is parked in front of the since-demolished Isle of Man Railway Co. Douglas carriage shed on 5th February 1994. *(Richard Dodge)*

Joining the twelve short Reeve Burgess and Plaxton-bodied Dennis Darts during 1994/1995 were a further ten to the 9.8m specification, capable of seating 40 (14/15/72-79 – MAN 14A[ii], MAN 15D[ii], CMN 72-79X). Passengers are ready to board Dart 78 on 28th June 1997 whilst it was working the short-lived route 10 extension to Tynwald Craft Valley.*(Richard Dodge)*

Although the majority of the single-deck fleet had already been replaced, IOMT received 25 further Dennis Darts during 1997, of the low-floor SLF configuration with Marshall bodywork, 16-40 (DMN 16-20R[i], DMN 21-30R, DMN 31R[i], DMN 32-40R). They were acquired in connection with the ill-fated 'New-bus-network', a plan for a completely revised Island bus system which provoked criticism and condemnation from various parties - the scheme being cancelled soon after the arrival of David Howard. Finished in a new-style 'coke-can' livery with Easyrider branding, these Darts were effectively to oust youthful non-low-floor Darts and, in turn, all bar eleven of the 'Easyriders' were also disposed of prematurely. Bus 17 heads a line of sister vehicles at Douglas Railway Station on 18th October, 1997 - all yet to enter traffic. *(Richard Dodge)*

Over the years the Manx bus fleet has contained several historic and significant vehicles, perhaps no more so than the final double-deck chassis produced by both AEC and Bristol manufacturers. Whilst the AEC - 410 LMN - was new to Douglas Corporation, the final Olympian built at the Bristol factory was one of a number of second-hand Olympians acquired by IOMT during the mid 1990's. Parked at Douglas Sea Terminal the two 'lasts' are seen on August 4, 2001, shortly before 57 (MAN 57N) was sold for preservation in the UK. By this date the Olympian was wearing the red and cream livery adopted following the arrival of David Howard as Transport Director in 1999 - this being an adaptation of that worn by his previous employer, Eastbourne Buses. *(Richard Dodge)*

In addition to the 25 new Dennis Dart SLFs, IOMT also acquired nine youthful 1989/1990 ex-Halton Transport all-Leyland Lynxes, 89-97 (MAN 89-94F, MAN 95-97N), creating a predominantly single-deck fleet. Prior to being prepared for vehicle examiner inspection Lynx 94 sits on top of the steam cleaning pit at Douglas railway yard on 18th November 1997, still in Halton livery which differed little from IOMT's own of the period. *(Richard Dodge)*

A change of direction occurred after the 'Smith' era ended and the 'Howard' period commenced, not only with another new livery, but more significantly it marked a switch back to double-deckers for the fleet. Orders for new low-floor 'deckers were placed and 14 former Stagecoach Selkent 1985 ECW-bodied Leyland Olympians were purchased in late 1999/early 2000 becoming IOMT 3-13/44/46/47 (EMN 203-13U, MAN 44U, MAN 46/47F), having been converted to single-door layout prior to delivery. Last of the 14 to arrive, 47, is seen at Circus Beach, Douglas on 20th February 2000 having just arrived on the Island and still carrying its UK identity C98 CHM. *(Richard Dodge)*

Delivery of IOMT's new low-floor double-deck buses started in early summer 2000 when East Lancs-bodied Dennis Tridents 48-53 (EMN 48-53Y) appeared on the Manx roads. Numerically the first, 48, passes the Manx Arms bus stop, Onchan on 24th June 2000 on route 15 to Ramsey, just days prior to the long established route number being changed to 3. *(Richard Dodge)*

The last of the second-hand Leyland Olympians were purchased during 2003, in the shape of five ex-Dublin Bus Alexander (Belfast)-bodied examples new in 1990. These buses replaced five 1997 Marshall-bodied Dennis Dart SLFs and, unusually, received the fleet and registration numbers from the Darts they replaced - 16-20 (DMN 16-20R[ii]), although 16 had been renumbered 46 prior to entry into service. Parked alongside IOMT's Banks Circus Headquarters at Douglas Railway Station, Olympian 19 shows off its ungainly tree deflector, today an essential fitment after the growth of foliage throughout the Island, especially over the last twenty years. *(Barry Edwards)*

Although he left a not entirely happy legacy for IOMT's vintage railways, David Howard did achieve a well presented largely modern bus fleet and good route network. This April 2007 view clearly shows just how the fleet has changed from its darkest days of the 1980's with a line of East Lancs-bodied DAFs 4/7 (GMN 615E, 71E), Marshall-bodied Dennis Dart SLF 30 (DMN 22R) and Northern Counties-bodied Leyland Olympians 60/65 (BMN 60V, 65P) at Douglas railway yard. *(Barry Edwards)*

IOMT East Lancs-bodied Alexander Dennis Trident II 17 (HMN 220A) pauses at the Laxey Glen Gardens bus stop on 12th June 2009 with fleetnames removed in readiness for rebranding with 'Bus Vannin' logos. A recent development shows some destinations displayed in Manx Gaelic or Manx & English, perhaps useful for those who speak the language as their natural tongue but sometimes confusing to tourists. *(Richard Dodge)*

Many Manx buses have attained long service lives, perhaps in part due to the traditionally seasonal nature of much of the operation. This is less true today and, with easier transport access to and from the Island following the introduction of Ro-Ro services by Manx Line and IOM Steam Packet, buses are often shipped to the UK at an earlier age. It was less usual for buses from the pre-war period to find a use outside the Island, but the chassis of former DCT 1923 Tilling-Stevens 10 (MN 2615) was acquired by the British Transport Commission during 1957 and has since been displayed at various museums. The chassis is seen at London Transport's Covent Garden Museum on September 7, 1994. *(Richard Dodge)*

Many vehicles, in pre Ro-Ro days, found further uses on the Island after withdrawal from service including former Douglas Corporation 1936 Leyland Cub 10 (BMN 256), which spent many years as an immobile toilet at Great Meadow racecourse, where it is seen during 1985, albeit by then disused. *(Richard Davis)*

Hiding in the undergrowth at Regaby during October 2007 is former Isle of Man National Transport 10 (E156 MAN), an ex-Ribble Motor Services Leyland Leopard with Marshall bodywork. Regaby had been home for the Leopard since 1983 but, after some attention, it was driven away to a new lease of life in preservation. *(Richard Davis)*

Leopard 10, travelling on trade-plates, makes good its escape from captivity. Note the non-standard features such as curtains, chimney etc. It might not look much but 10 had a new engine fitted in 1983 and it had only done about 1200 miles before the bus was withdrawn from service. *(Richard Davis)*

One of the more colourful all-over adverts to feature in the IOM Passenger Transport Board fleet was applied to former Merseyside PTE Alexander-bodied Leyland Atlantean 55 (MAN 3264), which had been made to resemble an Isle of Man Railway train and titled 'The Train Bus'. After withdrawal by 23rd June 1990, the bus passed to the IOM Fire Service for staff exercises before its remains were towed to Kirk Michael for scrap on 30th November 1991. (Richard Dodge)

Withdrawn from service in July 2001, Leyland Lynx BMN 401T, formerly IOM Transport 1, is seen in its new role as an airside bus at Ronaldsway Airport on 27th August 2003. The garish red and yellow colour scheme has since been replaced by all-over white. (Barry Edwards)

One of the 1975 ex-Grampian/South Yorkshire Leyland Nationals, imported by IOM Passenger Transport in 1986, ends its days as a rusting hulk at Bride in January 2007. *(Richard Davis)*

Operated by the IOM Department of Education as the Schools Computer Bus, MAN 30N, originally IOM National Transport 30 (and the last National to be withdrawn) has been carefully and properly maintained and looks very good after 30 years of use. The scene is a vintage vehicle rally at Jurby on 22nd July 2007 with National 32, currently under restoration, in the background. *(Barry Edwards)*

Vintage transport on the old Jurby parade ground, July 2007, probably the largest gathering of preserved buses ever assembled on the Island. It was opened by the then Minister for Tourism and Leisure Mr. Adrian Earnshaw MHK (on the right, dressed in a sleeveless shirt) who drove the 1928 Thornycroft BC Forward, far left of the picture, on a lap of the parade ground. *(Barry Edwards)*

The former IOM Road Services Homefield works was replaced by a new transport headquarters and workshops at Douglas railway yard (Banks Circus) during 1999, since when it has been used for storing heritage rail and bus stock. The remaining buses were removed during Spring 2009, with the last bus to leave being, appropriately, the oldest surviving IOMRS bus - 1927 Leyland Lion MN 5105. Attached to the tow-truck the Lion is about to be taken from the building on Thursday, 12th March bound for its new home at the Jurby Transport Museum. *(Richard Davis)*

Former IOM Road Services' Leyland Titan PD3 32 (XMN 346) on tow at Ballaquayle Road, Douglas, beginning its journey to Jurby on Wednesday, 11th March 2009. Out of shot, to the left of the photographer, is the site of the former Douglas Corporation cable tramway and bus depot. *(Richard Davis)*

20th March 2009 - another exhibit for Jurby is the last surviving Road Services Leyland/MCW Olympic, dating from 1951 - believed to be one of only three of the type still existing world-wide. *(Richard Davis)*

During March and April 2009 Isle of Man Transport took delivery of eleven Wright Eclipse Gemini-bodied Volvo B9TL double-deckers, 60-70 (JMN 46-56R), introducing both body and chassis types previously not seen in the fleet. Finished in East Yorkshire Motor Services' maroon and cream livery they introduced the fleetname 'Bus Vannin'. Within weeks of entry into service the buses were renumbered 160-170 as shown by 168 picking up passengers in Laxey on 9th June, 2009, working route 3B to Rhumsaa (Ramsey). (Richard Dodge)

4th August 2009 marked the end of the Leyland era for the Island's scheduled bus services with all bar two being withdrawn. (Two Northern Counties versions being retained as a back-up for schools use). The two final Olympians 83 and 99, with appropriate lettering, are seen shortly after their final runs, parked in the bus yard adjacent to Douglas Railway Station. Both were moved to Jurby Transport Museum on permanent loan later the same week. (Richard Davis)